Easy Star
BIOGRAPHIES

MEET Olivia Rodrigo!

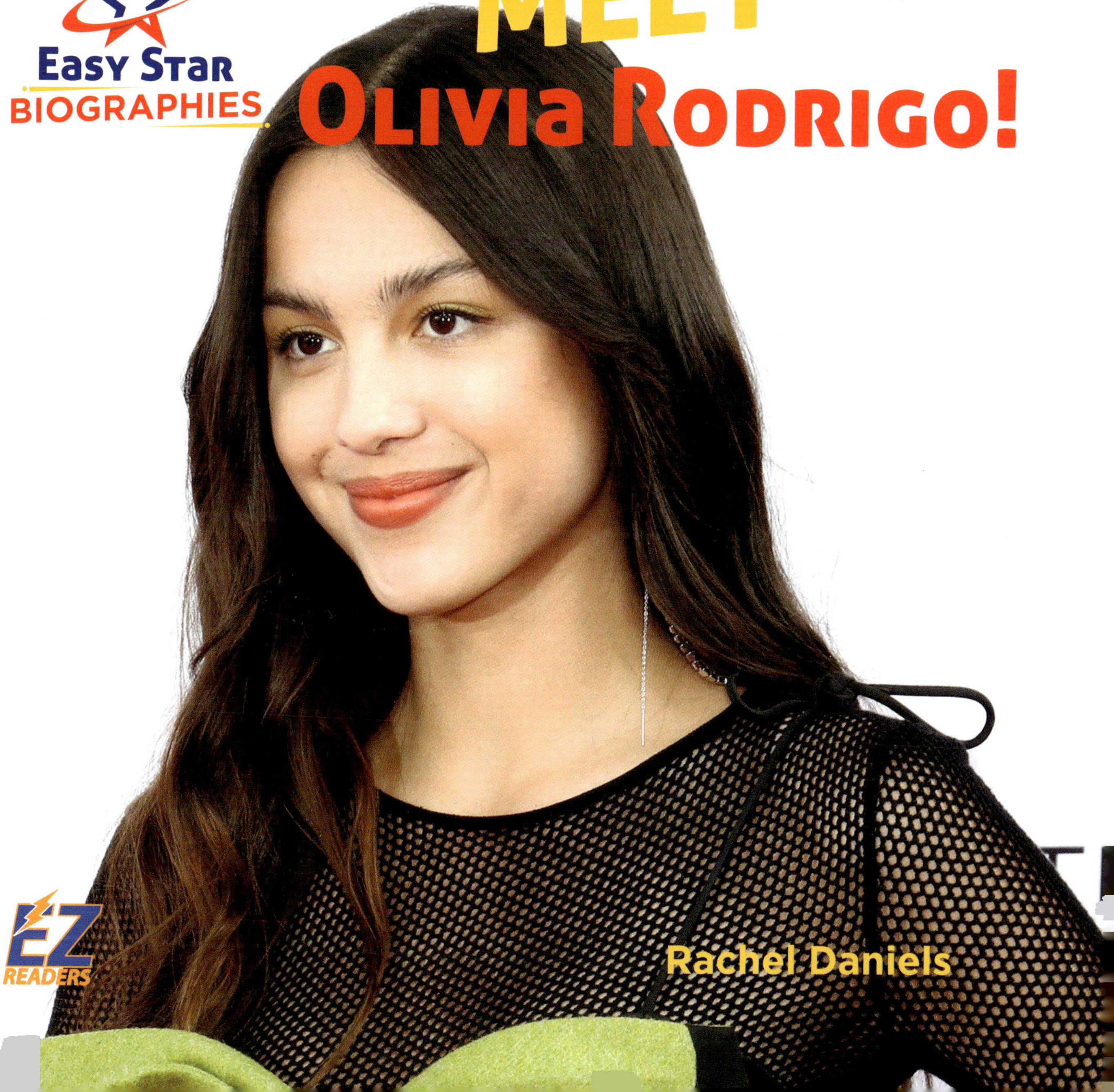

Rachel Daniels

EZ READERS

Creating Young Nonfiction Readers

EZ Readers lets children delve into nonfiction at beginning reading levels. Young readers are introduced to new concepts, facts, ideas, and vocabulary.

Tips for Reading Nonfiction with Beginning Readers

Talk about Nonfiction
Begin by explaining that nonfiction books give us information that is true. The book will be organized around a specific topic or idea, and we may learn new facts through reading.

Look at the Parts
Most nonfiction books have helpful features. Our *EZ Readers* include a Contents page, an index, and color photographs. Share the purpose of these features with your reader.

Contents
Located at the front of a book, the Contents displays a list of the big ideas within the book and where to find them.

Index
An index is an alphabetical list of topics and the page numbers where they are found.

Photos/Charts
A lot of information can be found by "reading" the charts and photos found within nonfiction text. Help your reader learn more about the different ways information can be displayed.

With a little help and guidance about reading nonfiction, you can feel good about introducing a young reader to the world of *EZ Readers* nonfiction books.

Mitchell Lane
PUBLISHERS

2001 SW 31st Avenue
Hallandale, FL 33009
www.mitchelllanepub.com

First Edition, 2025.

Author: Rachel Daniels
Designer: Ed Morgan
Editor: Morgan Brody

Easy Star Biographies: Meet Olivia Rodrigo!
Mitchell Lane Publishers
Hallandale, FL 33009

Library bound ISBN: 979-8-89260-125-2
eBook ISBN: 979-8-89260-131-3
Paperback ISBN: 979-8-89260-150-4

EZ Readers is an imprint of Mitchell Lane Publishers.

Photo credits: Alamy

CONTENTS

Olivia is a singer.

She was born in California.
She began to sing at age 8.

She writes songs.

She was a TV star.

She loves cats.

She is known for her **kindness**.

Her favorite color is purple.
Olivia loves popcorn.

Fans like her music.
Fans like her look.

She has won **awards**.

fast facts

- Olivia's real name is Olivia Isabel Rodrigo.
- She enjoys a **vegan** diet.
- She loves to eat SkinnyPop popcorn.
- Her favorite number is nine.
- She is afraid of birds.
- Her debut single was *drivers license*.
- Another popular song is *Vampire*.

key dates

2003	Olivia Rodrigo is born February 20 in California.
2009	Olivia starts acting.
2019	Stars in the TV show *High School Musical*.
2021	She debuts her first single *drivers license*.
2021	Wins MTV Award for Top New Artist.
2021	Named "Entertainer of the Year" by *Time* magazine.
2022	Wins **Grammy** for Best New Artist Vocal.

glossary

awards (UH-wardz)
Honor

debut (day-BYOO)
The first appearance

Grammy (GRA-mee)
An award for music

kindness (kined-nuhs)
Being gentle, caring, and helpful

look (luk)
Fashion style

vegan (VEE-gn)
A person who does not eat anything that comes from an animal

read more

Schwartz, Heather E. *Olivia Rodrigo: Hit Singer-Songwriter*. Minneapolis, MN: Lerner Publications. 2022.

index